13 YOUNG MEN

How
Charles E. Smith
Influenced a
Community

by
DAVID BRUCE SMITH

ISBN no. 978-0-615-26854-5
First Impression

For Alexandra, Max, Stacy, and Michael

Author's Note:

Some of the information within — based on conversations — has been converted to letters and memos to vary the presentation of the material.

Do one thing every day that scares you.

…Eleanor Roosevelt

The great use of life is to spend it for something that outlasts it.

…William James

Prologue

Dear David,

By the time you read this, I will be gone, but not far, because I believe there will be a Hereafter.

All of your life I have looked after you, and every day for the rest of your life I will continue to do so from the Beyond. You asked me once, "What if there is no Beyond?"

I believe that after a complex experience such as life, something must follow. If I'm wrong, well then, we've just had a few entertaining conversations about it that no one will know about.

I expected to live to be 100 years, but G-d is going to take me sooner; I don't know why I feel this way, but I do. Something in my bones, something in my inner self tells me that I will not have the party of all parties—my 100th birthday. I will miss you; I will miss seeing Alexandra grow; I will miss knowing Max. But, you must be strong because I will watch you and them and the rest of the family.

You will eventually find a letter that I wrote to Alexandra somewhere within my things at the office. You must read it to her so that she will know about me, my past, our family beliefs and our values. I hope—if I am able—to write a similar letter to Max. If I cannot, ask him not to be hurt or insulted. My memory is so bad now and

I don't know how long it will last. I hope, dear Grandson, that I do not forget you. But if I do, always know that I have loved you.

While I am able, I must ask you a favor because you are the family historian. We have written three books together, but the story of how I and others raised the necessary funds to build the Hebrew Home, the Jewish Social Service Agency building and the Jewish Community Center in Rockville has never been told. Nor has the story about how I became interested in Jewish education for Jewish survival. I believe that these things would be of interest to many people, but I fear that if you do not write it, no one will. Too many good things get forgotten because they're not written down. There are many times I wish I had kept a diary or a journal but I have no aptitude for it.

Please do this for me, Grandson. Remember "The Three Circles of Life" which I told you about in Phoenix many years ago? Family always comes first, followed by friends, and then the community.

This is my advice to you—but not all of it as you will see from the letters I have left you.

If G-d allows it, I will re-appear from time to time.

I love you,
Papa Charlie

Part One

A Wave of Judaism

Chapter One

Jewish Community Center, Rockville, Maryland

"We have gathered this afternoon to lay with appropriate ceremony and solemnity the cornerstone of a temple. The splendid structure which is to rise here will be the home of the Jewish Community Center of Washington."

President Calvin Coolidge, 1925

In 1911, 17 [1] Jewish teenagers convened a meeting of the Young Men's Hebrew Association in Washington, D.C.

During the next decade-and-a-half, sports, health, and cultural events expanded to various spots in the city.

In 1925, President Calvin Coolidge attended the laying-of-the-cornerstone ceremonies for the District of Columbia Jewish Community Center (DCJCC) at 16th and Q Streets, N.W. The following year the building was opened. And, it flourished. Maurice Bisgyer, the first Executive Director, held his position from 1924-1937; Paul Goldblatt succeeded him for the 1937-1938 season, and Edward Rosenbloom reigned from 1938-1958.

The DCJCC was the place to augment one's Jewish identity; it administered a consistent and conscientious collection of classes in music, art, dance, and languages; it was also a "comfort zone"— of sorts — where Jews could reinforce — with ease — their dedication and observance of the traditions.

Thirty years into the Center's existence, it had 813 members and a monthly visitor attendance of 2,500. Of that

---

[1] Most of the quoted statistics come from papers written by Stephen A. Mihm, Roberta Benor, and Robert Weiner. See bibliography for additional details.

total, 300 came daily to use the health club; at the time a family membership cost $30 per year.

But simultaneous to that growth — and not immediately apparent — was a change in participation that was partially influenced by the Roosevelt administration. The New Deal attracted Jewish scientists, social workers, lawyers, and accountants.

These eclectic jobs provided higher pay, an unexpected economic lift out of the lower middle class, and an enticement to move to the Maryland suburbs where larger tracts of relatively inexpensive land were available.

A 1956 study by Stanley K. Bigman revealed that 49.9% of the Jews lived in the Maryland and Virginia suburbs while 50.1% resided in the District. In addition, 75% of those families with children under the age of 17 were expected to move to Montgomery County, Maryland.

By 1959 the United States Government was employer to approximately 30 percent of the area's 80,000-90,000 Jews.

If "temptation" is what propelled a kind of exodus, it appears to have commenced in the mid-1940s and peaked in the late 1960s. In the meantime, the District's demographics spun significantly. Dwellings formerly owned by whites were purchased by poorer blacks; nascent crime escalated and the racial wheel was turned up. Much of the up-until-now tamped down tension oozed, destructively. Jews stopped attending the Center in large numbers—or began to leave for home before dark—and by April, 1968, Washington, D.C. was immersed in Black-White war.

These dynamics-in-process were not unnoticed by the Board of the Jewish Community Center (JCC), yet significant action was constantly postponed. Most of the directors were elderly and had stringent loyalties to dated points of view. Some urged for the sale of 16th and Q in favor of another edifice in the suburbs, but the majority pushed only for a theoretical suburban satellite office disguised as a center—of sorts.

A new, young, and experienced Executive Director named Robert Weiner was selected in 1958 to replace the retiring Edward Rosenbloom. He had a variegated and sophisticated career in Jewish Community Center management in Buffalo, New York and San Antonio, Texas. But, he was quickly frustrated by 16th and Q's Board; one member had already teased him that "the average age of the Board was 'deceased!'" [2]

An incident that occurred in an October, 1958, Board meeting convinced its president, Morton Wilner, that younger leadership was needed. While the budget for 1959 was being reviewed, one of the established members questioned every line item, and indicated he was dissatisfied with the

---

[2]Stephen A. Mihm, "Maintaining a Jewish Presence in the Nation's Capital: The Debate over the Location and Function of the District Jewish Community Center", July 19, 1993, p. 7.

proposed numbers. After the session was over, Weiner queried the gentleman about his rancor. The gentleman replied,

"I don't like newcomers telling us what to do."

Weiner, thinking that that director was attacking him, defended himself by saying that being new had nothing to do with the preparation of the budget. The Board member stated that he was referring to the presenter. "But the presenter has been a member of the Board for almost twenty-five years," Weiner reminded him. "I know," the director agreed, "but I've been on the Board for thirty-five years!"

A new committee was formed, immediately. Chaired by Leo Schlossberg, it recommended a swift change in the By-Laws. On December 15, 1958 an amendment was passed that would read:

"Upon completion of 21 years of continuous service as a member of the Board of Directors, said member shall, at the expiration of his elected term, thereupon automatically become an Honorary Member of the Board for life with the same status as all other members of the board."

Three years later the Center had a new roster of administrators.

⸺⤫⸺

Between the late 1950s and the mid-1960s, 16th and Q spent much of its time vying for an appropriate place and destiny within the community. The Board recognized the neighborhood was deteriorating, but diluted the organization's advancement with endless discourse about what the neighborhood would look like in 25 years hence — the 1970s and beyond. Unsure and unable to prognosticate, they went with the logic that "it was better to be inadequately located for everybody than to be conveniently located for a few." [3]

Perhaps thinking it could beat back obsolescence inexpensively, the DCJCC approved a modest renovation that would create gallery space to showcase eight exhibitions per year with accompanying lectures, build new meeting rooms, make modest mechanical upgrades, and inaugurate an outreach program to various synagogues that would provide professional services to Temple youth groups. The Center also moved its day camp—located on the roof—to Green Acres School in Rockville, MD, causing an enrollment spike from 60 to 250 children. These changes generated an immediate increase in membership. The figures from 1958 zenithed from 800 to 3,014 in November of 1960.

But the euphoria proved to be temporary. Summer 1959 at-

[3]Mihm, p. 9.

tendance at the teenage dances declined from 300 to approximately 50; a YMCA had opened in Silver Spring, Maryland, as had a private swim club in Arlington, VA.

Large numbers of families were continuing to flow northward. Maryland was now perceived as The Place to Be. A telephone survey from the early 1960s corroborated the now conspicuous and undesirable trend on-the-rise: parents did not want their children at 16th and Q in the evenings. Because of this, some programming was transferred to Eastern Junior High School in Silver Spring, MD, but it was largely unsuccessful, because "in a public school they [the students] felt no sense of identification with either the Center or the Jewish Community." [4] Even with a $55,900 allocation from the United Givers Fund, the Center was unable to expand its services or its reach.

So, now, with no reliably attended Center, paired with the inability of the synagogues to afford youth programming, there emerged a 1962 wave of "pre-delinquent" behavior. Within three months, 80 Jewish teenagers were picked up by the authorities. A report from the time reveals that the adolescents were not a part of a gang or restricted to a neighborhood or economic stratum. All of them had either stolen cars, deflated tires, or committed some sort of low level destruction because "they had nothing else to do."

And, they were bored.

---

[4]Robert H. Weiner, The Jewish Community Center of Greater Washington, 1958-1983 – Years of Change, 1983, p. 6.

The post-Calvin Coolidge — 16th and Q Street dream had been achieved at an impressive clip that somehow meandered. The Center's tentacles of cultural influence had drifted, and its remaining sources of revenue—athletics and rooftop dances—were inadequate for long-term survival.

Chapter Two

1964

Mrs. Morton Rabineau, Chairman,
reported that the following slate will be submitted
to the Center's Annual Meeting:

President:
Charles E. Smith

Vice-Presidents:
Bernard Gewirz, Responsible for Budget
Mrs. Morton Rabineau, Responsible for Program
Maurice Shapiro, Responsible for Membership

Treasurer:
Henry Reich

Assistant Treasurer:
Sheldon S. Cohen

Recording Secretary:
Max S. Gross

Corresponding Secretary:
Mrs. Harold Kramer

January 2, 1990

Dear David,

*I became President of the Board of the District of Columbia
Jewish Community Center in June of Nineteen Hundred
and Sixty-four. And, as I recall, people were scared to go
there because of the crime. I remember very clearly that
during one of our meetings someone threw a brick
through the window. Fortunately, no one was hurt.*

*Thousands of people were still interested in the idea of
having a Center, but at that time we were losing some of
our membership. But, as you know from our many talks, I
hadn't yet presented my vision for the Hebrew Home for
the Aged in Rockville, Maryland. Later on I added the
Jewish Community Center and the Jewish Social Service
Agency buildings. Eventually, that campaign would
change everything.*

*Besides the difficulties with the neighborhood which we
faced in the District, most Jews were moving to the
suburbs, and the existing Center was considered too far
away. Remember: the roads from Maryland to Washington
were not so developed then.*

*I had an idea — a vision — that I was going to present to
the Board, but I did not know how it would be received. It
would be later in the year. And boy oh boy did I hear it
from the community then!*

*Let me tell you what I said when I started my term on
June 23rd:*

"Fifty-one percent of the Washington Jewish community lives in Montgomery County, MD— and we have a tiny bungalow to accommodate them. We must build a branch Jewish Community Center in Montgomery County to meet the needs of the Jewish families that live there. It is our duty. It is our responsibility."

I told them that: "We must inspire in our children and grandchildren a love for Judaism and provide a better Jewish education. We must provide better care and supervision for our aged and sick. Our community must have a center — where in a Jewish environment a play, recreation, and cultural programs can be permeated with Jewish content. We must make a concerted move to train Jewish leaders."

And: "We must furnish our young people with a proper environment, facilities, and equipment so that they will want to come and participate. We must make them proud of their leaders and their Jewish community. This should be our goal."

You may want to shorten this. I'll leave the decision to you.

Love,
Papa Charlie

Not long after Papa Charlie's appointment, Jewish Social Service Agency (JSSA) President, Richard England, alongside nine members of his and the JCC Boards, made an inspection of 16th and Q which disclosed its compromised condition:

There are many walls with bad leaks and large sections of plaster have dropped off. The only elevator is slow and uncertain. The heating plant is obsolete and there is no central air conditioning. There is a constant problem with rats and roaches. In some areas there are actual holes in the floor, covered by small metal plates to keep people from falling through. One of the most glaring evidences of this is in the main auditorium, which is rented on Saturday nights to Negro youth groups in order to provide some income for the Center. I believe this produces about $100 each evening it is rented. Jewish children simply do not want to be in that neighborhood in the evening, and so this rental arrangement produces some good from an otherwise empty room.

Illustrative of the fact that there is such an enormous demand for the Jewish Community Center's type of services in Montgomery County, is the fact that a tiny bungalow in the center of Silver Spring has been loaned temporarily to the Center. Since there was no money available to fix up the house, the children themselves performed all the labor of cleaning and repainting. The house is built to accommodate a very small family, two adults and two children. Although only about 40 children can be squeezed into the house at any one time, approximately 350 different children use this house every week. The reason for this intense usage is because the house is located in a safe neighbor-

22

hood where Jewish children can get to easily. Almost no Jewish children go downtown to the Center except on Sundays. Even then, only a small handful participate.

∞∞∞

Papa Charlie's vision eventually shifted into a relocation of the Jewish Community Center, the Jewish Social Service Agency, and the Hebrew Home into three adjacent buildings to a campus-like setting in Maryland. Because a majority of Jews were already settled in Montgomery County, that area seemed to be the most sensible place to be.

The Executive Directors of the Agencies, Sam Roberts of the Hebrew Home, George Pikser of the Jewish Social Service Agency, and Robert H. Weiner of the Jewish Community Center (JCC), approved of the concept, but large portions of the three boards did not. A number of Papa Charlie's friends were opposed to his idea because it was perceived to be preposterous, formidable, difficult, expensive, and mostly—unattainable.

Elder leadership did not believe sufficient funds could be raised to absorb the costs of the ground and infrastructure. And: the axiomatic philosophy that it would be "one thing to abandon Cleveland, Ohio, or Detroit...but you can't abandon the nation's capital." [5]

---

[5]Mihm, p. 14.

23

These men — some older than my grandfather — further argued that Maryland was too remote; wages were higher, and there was a generalized anxiety about whether District health care workers would be amenable to a longer, more expensive commute to a new facility.

That powerful clique also believed that doctors would oppose a relocation; they were satisfied that the existing home on Spring Road in Washington, D.C. was filled—with a waiting list. But, Papa Charlie did not have faith in any of their objections. The number of Jewish residents in the District was much lower than in Maryland.

When my grandfather presented his plan to the Board at the Jewish Community Center, they said,

"Why waste time on something that cannot be accomplished?"

The Hebrew Home said they would remain in the District; the Jewish Social Service Agency Board voted against him— unanimously.

After those rejections, Papa Charlie went to the United Givers Fund for assistance, but they discouraged him. The largest amount of money they had ever raised was $500,000 in 1953 for an addition to the Home, but mostly, they feared a community center campaign would conflict with their annual capital drive of $1.5 million.

Still, my grandfather believed the three groups needed only more evidence to persuade them that his vision made sense. And so, with a small committee of Board members, and 16th and Q's Robert Weiner, he visited other Jewish Hebrew Homes for the Aged in New York, Detroit, Los Angeles, Cleveland, Buffalo, Oakland, Seattle, Richmond, and Ottawa, Canada.

Papa Charlie viewed Jewish Community Centers in Baltimore, Cleveland, Kansas City, St. Louis and Richmond. And, he questioned the fundraisers: What makes for a successful drive? How should the plan be pursued? Is it feasible to build three buildings at once? They told him that if he could find a solid core of support—approximately 60 percent of the total amount—the remainder could be raised in smaller amounts from within the Jewish community. Because Papa Charlie knew so many of the prosperous Jews in Washington—and had even had a part in their successes—he believed they would provide the majority of the financial compensation.

By October, Papa Charlie and his group had a completed feasibility study, alongside a prodigious portfolio of facts.

He returned to the Jewish Community Center. This time, the directors voted up a motion to build a larger, more modern facility in a suburban location.

The Jewish Social Service Agency also came around to concurrence. Now, my grandfather needed an alliance with the toughest of the three boards: the conservative, and more religious, Hebrew Home.

But, before a return visit, Papa Charlie suggested to Executive Director Sam Roberts that the two of them meet with 12 residents to explain what was envisioned for them in a new building. They told each of the selected persons that their plan was to construct an up-to-date building with single and double rooms, private bathrooms, air conditioning, and that it would be located in a park-like setting conducive to walks.

The first man told Roberts and my grandfather, "I am opposed to it." They asked, "Wouldn't you like a private bath?"

"No, at night I go down the hall, do what I have to do, and go back to sleep."

The next resident was asked, "Don't you want air conditioning?" And she responded, "I hate air conditioning."

Each of the other ten residents was also contrary, which Papa Charlie reported to the Board.

The facility was voted down.

Some weeks later, Papa Charlie called on his friend, Samuel P. Cohen, president of the Home, and told him that the ground he was planning to build on would be large enough to accommodate the three agencies. My grandfather informed Cohen he was going to present the strategy to the Home one more time. If they turned him down again, he would still pursue his intention to erect a new Community Center.

Papa Charlie knew the Home was larger than the Jewish Community Center, and he suspected that Cohen would ob-

ject to having an agency like it take the position of an up-
start against his.

"Charlie," Cohen replied, "I'll be damned if I'm gonna let the
tail wag the dog!"

At the next Board meeting, Cohen made a forceful argu-
ment in favor of a new building, pointing out that the present Home was old, and in poor condition. When he finished,
a motion was made to proceed, and it passed.

January 16, 1990

My dear David,

*Let's go back so you can follow this. I remember most of
it because I have my papers in front of me.*

*The night I was installed as the President of the Jewish
Community Center, I told the Board a number of things.
First: Washington was the 6ᵗʰ largest metropolitan center
of Jewish population, with approximately 90,000 Jews.
Yet, only 3,800 belonged to the DCJCC—less than 4.5%! This
was very unsatisfactory to me.*

*Some people might have thought, 3,800 was a big
number, but I told them if we need an example of what a
revitalized, dynamic JCC can be and do, we needed to look*

at other cities such as Pittsburgh, where almost a quarter of the Jewish population—10,500 out of 47,000 people—belonged to the JCC. Or St. Louis, Missouri, where 20% belong—12,000 out of 60,000. In Baltimore, they had 10,800 members that kept their new 1960 building busy. Its 76,000 square foot structure was located on three acres of well-landscaped ground, including parking for 230 cars.

I told them that as soon as the Baltimore people moved into their new Center in 1960, memberships soared. They had 10,000 very active members and five times more usage out of their facilities than before. As a matter of fact, they had a real problem because their building was designed to accommodate 6,000 and they already had 4,000 more members than they technically had room for.

Later, when I visited Baltimore with a few other men, we arrived at noon. Every parking place was full, as was practically every room and facility. Everything looked clean, modern, and crowded. Nearly every aspect of cultural, and athletic, and recreational life was taken care of: a 35' X 75' swimming pool with folding bleachers for use during swim meets; a complete cafeteria and even a private dining room where we had lunch with members of their Board; a huge gymnasium; elaborate facilities for staging plays and concerts, and private rooms for use by 500 members of the Golden Age Club.

People are attracted to the new—to the growing—to

the successful, I reminded them. Baltimore's new building
and increasing membership was in turn stimulating new
membership, whereas Washington's decrepit facilities
could only make prospective members think twice.

I told them I believed that we live in a community
where our resources far exceed our needs, and if we
failed, it will only be because we have become complacent,
indifferent, unconcerned, and strangers to our heritage.

While other communities were growing, all we had
managed to accumulate was a deficit of $27,000.

David, we actually could not pay our creditors and I
showed them the bills.

Love,
Papa Charlie

Chapter Three

1965

The Advisory Board, Hebrew Home

Throughout the year there were questions, discussions, and a profusion of debates.

A survey that explained the prospective complex was assembled and mailed to the 112 board members of the agencies; 93 replies were received. Momentum was in process outside of the board rooms.

WHETHER TO MOVE?	VOTES
Yes	84
No	3
No Response	5
Question Not Answered	1

MOVE TO MONTROSE?	VOTES
Yes	64
In Favor of Larger Space	1
In Favor of Staying in DC	14
Remodel Existing Center	9
No Response	5

GO WITH MAJORITY?	VOTES
Yes	78
No	8
No Response	5
Question Not Answered	1

MORAL AND FINANCIAL SUPPORT?	VOTES
Yes	87
With Reservations	1
No	2
No Response	3

Thirty-seven of the same questionnaires were also sent to the Board of the Men's Club. Of the 21 returned replies, 20 voted for a new Hebrew Home, and one was returned unanswered.

A majority of the Hebrew Home employees said they would continue to work there even if the organization moved to Maryland.

Jewish Community Center
Of Greater Washington

M I N U T E S

Tuesday, March 15, 1965

Present: Dr. Ellis April, Norman Bernstein, David Bornet, Asher Ende, Stanley Frosh, Bernard Gewirz, Mrs. Aaron Goldman, Hymen Goldman, Ralph Goldsmith, Col. Julius Goldstein, Max Gross, Alexander Hassan, Joel S. Kaufmann, Robert P. Kogod, Mrs. Harold Kramer, Herman Neugass, Moe Offenberg, Rabbi Stanley Rabinowitz, Henry Reich, Stuart Werner, and Morton Wilner.

Staff: Col. B. J. Andruska, Philip M. Stillman, Al Tudor, and Robert H. Weiner.

Presiding: Charles E. Smith.

The meeting was called to order at 12:45 p.m. on March 15, 1965 by President Charles E. Smith.

Planning Committee

Asher Ende reported that two subcommittees had been formed and one, the Visitation Subcommittee, had already visited the Baltimore Jewish Community Center to meet and get ideas and learn pitfalls in the building of a new Center. He told the Board that a letter has been sent to every Jewish organization in the area advising them of the intentions of the

Jewish Community Center of Greater Washington and asking them for ideas on what the community needs that a Center can help with. The committee is now working on a series of written recommendations on the new building and the equipping of it.

Land Acquisition Committee

Norman Bernstein reported for the Land Acquisition Committee. The Committee has a site of 22 acres on Montrose Road which is available for about $27,000 per acre-and they recommend purchasing this site. Funds of about $150,000 would be required as a deposit.

The Land Acquisition Committee is authorized to purchase the 22-acre site on Montrose Road (known as Stock's Nursery) at a price not to exceed $588,000 after note discounts, under the best terms which can be negotiated. The Center is to purchase the land regardless of the decision made by the Board of the Hebrew Home for the Aged to join with us or not. The Center asks for six months to get zoning approval and for Mr. Smith to get loans from individuals to make the purchase. The President of the Center is hereby authorized to make any other arrangements necessary for such acquisition.

The motion passed unanimously.

In May, the campaign received even more horsepower:

THIRTEEN YOUNG MEN CONTRIBUTE ONE THOUSAND DOLLARS EACH TO START A 'BAR MITZVAH' LAND FUND

Monies will be used to pay for the future site of the Jewish Community Center and the Jewish Social Service Agency

Lawrence N. Brandt	Nathan Landow
Marvin Dekelboum	Gerald J. Miller
Joseph B. Gildenhorn	Alvin P. Ostrow
Marvin L. Kay	Charles Jay Pilzer
Lawrence Kirstein	Robert M. Rosenthal
Richard A. Kirstein	Robert H. Smith
Robert P. Kogod	

Two months later, Hyman Berman, president of the Home, reported that the site plan for the proposed complex had been completed, and the Advisory Committee made its recommendations which were to:

- **Move from Spring Road to a new location.**

- **Move to Montrose Road, Montgomery County, MD.**

- **Build a 250-bed facility as soon as funds can be raised {existing: 165 beds.}**

- **Capital fund drive should be done jointly with Jewish Community Center and Jewish Social Service Agency.**

- **Build the entire complex at one time.**

My grandfather also conceived the "Citizens' Committee" which, with the Board's endorsement, would be empowered to appoint subcommittees "including but not limited to a committee to evaluate community needs—a Site Committee, a Ways and Means Committee, and a Capital Funds Campaign Committee."

July 21, 1990

Dear David,

Somehow, I had to find a way to elevate thinking into giving, and to stimulate people to give generously, so I read some letters I had received from the six cities we had contacted. But, before I did that, I reminded the Board about what the cities of Toronto, Cleveland, Montreal, St. Louis, Detroit, and Baltimore had told us: their experiences had been that if the top 60 families of the city gave $31,000 each, the necessary $5,000,000 for the campaign could be raised.

Then, I proceeded to the letters. Better to let people <u>think</u> <u>a</u> <u>little</u> <u>more</u> <u>before</u> <u>they</u> <u>react</u>—especially when you're delivering news about money. Remember that, my Grandson. Most people are not born givers. You have to cultivate them along.

Anyway, the first letter I read was from San Diego, California, which commented on the outstanding "value of having {a} Home for Aged and JCC in such close proximity so that residents of the Home can participate in JCC activities...The second letter was from Youngstown, Ohio. They reported that "We have built our Home for the Aged on property which is contiguous to...our JCC. The third letter was from Flushing, New York, stating that there are savings on heating...utilities, dual use of facilities when not in use... {the} program lends itself towards integration of residents with community people and the integration of older adults with other age groups..."

Two doctors also wrote in. The first, Dr. Harold Dubin, was Dental Director of the Home; he did not predict any negative issues associated with a possible move or anticipate difficulties in staffing a dental clinic in Maryland. The last was from Dr. Harold L. Hirsh, Medical Director of the Home. He said: "The {medical} panel will continue in its present form. Most of the men on the panel already have offices in the suburban areas. Most of those that have offices in the District have Maryland licenses, and in any event there is an opportunity for temporary reciprocal arrangements for physicians serving in this capacity..."

After some more discussion, David, a motion was made — and passed without objection — to proceed with the Advisory Committee's recommendations.

I then formed a committee to supervise the sale of the Home, a committee to prepare and send out a community-wide newsletter, and I instructed our publicity director, Mrs. Sylvia Altman, to publicize the meeting results in the newspapers.

Love,
Papa Charlie

Soon, the architects, Cohen and Haft, were instructed to submit drawings to the Zoning Committee. For the time being the Center decided it would augment its D.C. operations by obtaining two properties on Q, one on 16th, and invest $30,000 in repairs and renovation. It still had 4,461 dues-paying members; most of them were only participating in suburban-based activities, but a majority of the health club aficionados resented the idea of a move, and would not contribute funds to the Rockville Campaign.

(Include in a future memoir?)

Notes from a July, 1965 meeting

... Board discussed an unsolicited $500,000 offer from the Washington Bible College to purchase the Center Building. We decided not to consider selling for a two-year period.

... I appointed Board Members Sheldon Cohen and Asher Ende to study and recommend the type of programs the Center might offer to attract the young Jewish Intellectual.

... Contract for the purchase of the land on Montrose Road has been signed. The architects are preparing preliminary plans which will be submitted by August 10th to secure the necessary zoning variance. Because the Hebrew Home Board has voted to build at the same time that the Center is constructed, I will call for a joint fundraising campaign.

(Notes for a memoir?)

In November of 1965, I established a Blue Ribbon
Committee to investigate the feasibility of having a
suburban complex—a campus that would combine
the Center, the Jewish Social Service Agency
(JSSA), and the Hebrew Home (HH). They are
presently located on Spring Road in Washington;
HH and JSSA are both dilapidated. The Home was
built in 1924. The HH is providing inadequate
service to an overflow of senior citizens who are
older than I am.

Chapter Four

Charles E. Smith
1101 17th Street, N.W.
Suite 1300
Washington, D.C. 20036

November 23, 1965

Mr. Hyman Berman
1730 Rhode Island Avenue, N.W.
Washington, D.C. 20036

Dear Hy,

I would like to express appreciation for your willingness to join us for dinner on Tuesday, November 30th at the Colonial Room of the Mayflower Hotel at 6 PM. A reservation has been made for you.

You might be interested to know that the response has been most satisfying and gratifying.

I am convinced that decisions of momentous importance will be reached which will benefit the Jewish Community for many years to come.

I am looking forward to seeing you on the 30th.

Cordially,

Charlie

Charles E. Smith
For the Organizing Committee

On November 30, Papa Charlie hosted 89 men for dinner at the Mayflower Hotel in Washington, D.C.

Family, friends, colleagues, and subcontractors showed; a decision had to be made about whether — or not — there would be a campaign to construct the Jewish Community Center Complex.

The agenda consisted of five minute speeches by various agency representatives and Milton Hood Ward, the company hired to assist in the fundraising. After they were finished, Papa Charlie noted that the prospective three buildings would be symbols of unity and Jewish values; committing to them, he believed, would be the most gratifying and meaningful event of his generation.

During the dinner, my grandfather quoted the Jewish writer Edward Joshinski who had died in a Communist prison:

> *"Never fear your friends. The most they can do is betray you. Never fear your enemies. The worst they can do is kill you. But always be fearful of the indifferent people. They are neither friends nor enemies. They will neither betray you nor kill you, but because of their indifference, hundreds of thousands of people have died."*

Papa Charlie told his audience that if they disagreed with him about fashioning the Complex, then he would respect their opinion. If they agreed, then they would proceed with the campaign. All he asked is that they not be indifferent.

After a few minutes of complete silence, his friend, Carl Freeman, stood and said: "Charlie, I support you in what you want to do and I will pledge $100,000." Papa Charlie said, "Carl, I am grateful for your support, but we're not soliciting funds tonight. I want everyone here to decide one way or another."

Within a few moments everyone rose.
My grandfather's eyes were teary, and the
campaign was begun.

November 30, 1965, Mayflower Hotel, Washington, DC

It was also decided that all of the funds would come from private sources, and there would be no mortgage. That night, The Greater Washington Jewish Community Foundation was formed to be the parent company to receive, hold, and administer the financial transactions.

The goal: $5,300,000.

Chapter Five

Mr. Charles E. Smith
4501 Connecticut Avenue, N.W.
Apartment 916
Washington, D.C. 20008

Dear David,

And so it began. The next day I started the campaign.
Within two weeks we had $2,000,000 so we fired the
fundraising organization hired from New York. They
didn't know the community; we decided we would do a
better job ourselves. I had my committee take several
cards each, call on several people, one at a time, and we
were very successful.

I could not have done this without Vivian Rabineau
and Alma Gildenhorn.

Love,
Papa Charlie

By the close of the year, approximately 20 sites had been toured and studied. Finally, the 22-acre "Stock's Nursery" on 6125 Montrose Road, Rockville, Maryland, was selected to be the location of the Complex. It was close to residential development, major highways, 3/10 of a mile from Rockville Pike, and it was viewed as a "magnet" for people living in a range of economic neighborhoods.

On December 30, 1965, the land was purchased by The Greater Washington Jewish Community Foundation. Construction would begin the following September.

1966

Jewish Community Center
of Greater Washington

Campaign Cabinet Committee

Mr. Hyman Berman

Mrs. Vivian Rabineau

Mr. Stanford Berman

Mr. Louis Grossberg

Mr. George Hurwitz

Mr. Cecil Kaufmann

Mr. Nat Paige

Mr. Joel Kaufmann

Mr. Jac Lehrman

Mr. Charles Jay Pilzer

Mr. Samuel P. Cohen

Mr. Jack Diamond

Mr. Pete Edles

Mr. Joseph Gildenhorn

Mr. Ralph Goldsmith

Mr. Herman Schechtel

Mr. Charles E. Smith

Mr. Martin Weil

Mr. Mort Wilner

The fundraising was targeted and intense. During the next four years my grandfather, Vivian Rabineau, Alma Gildenhorn, the Board, and hundreds of volunteers sent mailings to 4,000 families and solicited even more.

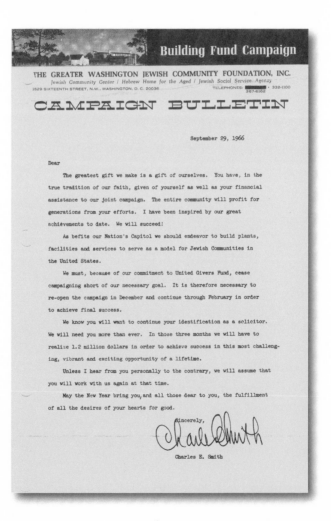

By January 11, 1966, 71 families had pledged a total of $2,939,000 of the $5,300,000 goal.

The fundraisers and Executive Directors that I talked to in Baltimore, Cleveland, Richmond and the other cities were correct about needing a core of major support. Within the average community, 60 families pledged 38% of the campaign total. In our community, 62 families pledged 63% of the $5,300,000.

As of May 18:

14 families pledged	$ 1,935,000	Avg. $ 138,000
48 families pledged	$ 1,414,250	Avg. $ 29,460
86 families pledged	$ 668,000	Avg. $ 7,700
83 families pledged	$ 131,770	Avg. $ 1,590
231	$ 4,149,020	$176,820

From the desk of...

Charles E. Smith

(Notes for a possible memoir?)

Because of rising costs, I am now projecting that we need one million dollars to complete the campaign. The first phase was a success. It will end on July 31st. We have performed a miracle: existence

A second phase will begin sometime in the fall so that it does not interfere with UGF's (United Givers Fund) fundraising. It will be conducted on 2 levels: Advanced Gifts of $1,000-$10,000 and General Solicitation of $1,000 gifts and down.

Structure of 2nd Phase

Advanced Gifts Division
2 Chairmen
12 Co-Chairmen
89 Vice Chairmen
103 LEADERS

General Solicitation Division
5 Chairmen
12 Co-Chairmen
170 Vice Chairmen
600 Captains
787 LEADERS

WISDOM: (for my grandchildren)
"When one must, one can."

--Yiddish Proverb

On August 18th: About $1,000,000 is still needed because of construction costs and square footage alterations.

On October 5th Vivian Rabineau reported on the fundraising campaign. The original goal of $5,300,000 has been passed; a new goal of $6,500,000 was set because the size of the projected buildings has been increased. This new goal has yet to be met. The fundraising campaign will go on actively in January and February of 1967. It is hoped to have the groundbreaking in March.

$5,360,000 has been raised as of today.

After January 1, each Board Member will be asked to see 2 people.

From the desk of...

CHARLES E. SMITH

(Possible wisdom to tell my grandchildren one day)

The tide was just right for the launching of the pioneer Jewish Community Complex.

As of Nov. 15, 1966 we raised $5,506,000.

We hope to renew our campaign Dec. 1, 1966 and successfully complete it by Mar. 1, 1967.

We owe all the wonderful men and women who have pledged a great debt of gratitude for their generosity and compassion. We have performed a great miracle. Let us pursue our labor of love to its ultimate conclusion and success.

WISDOM: "The difficult we do immediately; the impossible takes a little longer."

- motto of the U.S. Army Corps of Engineers, WWII

Chapter Six

THE GREATER WASHINGTON JEWISH COMMUNITY FOUNDATION

Honorary Chairmen

The Hon. Arthur J. Goldberg

The Hon. Abe Fortas

The Hon. Jacob Javitz

The Hon. Abraham A. Ribicoff

The Hon. David L. Bazelon

The Hon. Sheldon S. Cohen

The Hon. Lewis L. Strauss

Chairmen

Rabbi Isadore Breslau

Carl M. Freeman

David Lloyd Kreeger

Co-Chairmen

Samuel P. Cohen

Cecil D. Kaufmann

Joel S. Kaufmann

Jac J. Lehrman

Stanley H. Rosensweig

Charles E. Smith

So much still had to be done — and figured out. This was the biggest undertaking in the Washington Jewish community—ever.

Already it had been determined that the three buildings would be constructed simultaneously, and budgetary expenses would be allocated amongst the Complex.

Fundraising strategies and procedures had to be streamlined; incentives such as naming opportunities had to be organized, committees had to be fashioned to formulate comprehensive programming to originate membership fees; study groundbreaking plans and determine a date for the future dedication.

The Board decided that the principles of the drive would be:

To Define the Need by:

- *Creating the standards of the campaign — they could be either grandiose or lower than those set by another city.*

- *Determine what is really needed in the way of facilities and programming.*

- *Profit from the mistakes/successes of other communities.*

Develop a Community Perspective:

- *Is any other institution carrying on a capital funds drive, and if so, would this campaign depend on who they depend on?*

- *How ready are people to give?*

- *Various studies and visits to other communities had shown that drives of this sort attract big gifts that are pledged over 3-5 years.*

- *Naming opportunities are equally enticing because of people's desires to perpetuate their family names.*

- *Drive should not be concentrated on every level. It was believed that 500-600 families would give big gifts; the rest would be considered "gravy."*

- *People at the core of each institution had to be committed to give. If they were not pace setters, who would be?*

- *Capital fund drives do not substitute for annual giving; consultation with other Jewish Community Centers revealed that the two rarely cause conflict.*

From 1966 to 1968, Vivian Rabineau, now Vice-Chairman of the Board, convened a study commission. From the very beginning, she reminded the participants that because the buildings were to be debt-free, future generations would only have fiscal responsibility for the Center's programming.

And so, fifteen committees met regularly. Workbooks had to

be prepared and analyzed; then, recommendations were submitted about the types of activities the Center would tender to a medley of age constituencies: from nursery schoolers to retirees. Other task forces formulated cultural curricula in music, drama, dance, art, Judaism, and physical education.

A plethora of experts was also consulted: the Director of the Washington School of Ballet, authorities in Early Childhood Education at the University of Maryland, artists, a myriad of gallery owners, and Robin Wagner, who had designed one of the theatres at Lincoln Center in New York.

In their efforts to hone a nearly perfect Center, almost every detail was considered.

Roberta Benor, who authored "The Jewish Community Center of Greater Washington, 1958-1983: Twenty-Five Years of Service," observed "The commission asked probing questions. For example, with regard to the nursery school: What are the needs for a nursery school in the Jewish community? What currently are there in the way of nursery schools? What is it the Center wants to do? If there were a void in a certain area, the Center would try to fill it, but it didn't want to compete with the functions of the synagogues and other institutions." [6]

Robert Weiner, the Executive Director of the Jewish Community Center, recalled an equivalent amount of dedication to

---

[6] Roberta Benor, The Jewish Community Center of Greater Washington, 1958-1983: Twenty-Five Years of Service, p.5

the cause: "Each committee was to examine programs currently offered in their area of concentration to determine what was missing...first and foremost the Center's purpose was the survival of the Jewish people. Recommendations to the Board regarding the type and scope of the activities... came from 354 interested and concerned people." [7]

Eleven other groups—all administrative—were coordinated by Colonel Julius Goldstein. Alongside 156 experts in various fields, he and they developed house and membership rules as well as public relations and volunteer services. They outlined office, business, personnel, budget and maintenance procedures, and ways to obtain endowments.

According to Benor, approximately 50% of the Washington area Jews belonged to a synagogue; an even smaller number sent their children to a religious school.

"If the Center could make the Judaic atmosphere more attractive, then it could begin to educate, and that concept [would lead] to other things. The Center supplements and complements what the synagogues and day schools do." [8]

And so it did.

In a deliberate endeavor to further expand its potential reach into the community, the Board asked the Rabbinates for advice about *kashruth**, holiday closings, and other Judaic practices.

Kosher, according to Jewish dietary laws.

---

[7] Weiner, p. 9.
[8] Benor, pp. 5-6.

Initially, the Orthodox rabbis balked. They would not meet with the Conservative and Reform—"*the goyim*", they sneered. When it was learned that Saturday programming was under consideration, the Orthodox requested a meeting with the Board, and an agreement was crafted:

- *The Center would be closed on all Jewish holidays when there are services in synagogues.*

- *It would always be open on the 25ᵗʰ of December. If Chanukah occurred on that day, the JCC would celebrate it.*

- *The Center would observe kashruth, but it would be unsupervised by the Orthodox rabbinate.*

- *There would not be any children's activities on Sunday mornings.*

During Shabbat:

- *The Center would open at 2:00 P.M. to the public.*

- *The gym and pool would be open for individuals, but organized competition would be prohibited.*

- *No Jewish staff member would be required to work.*

- *A play could be performed, but no tickets could be sold.*

- *Phone calls would not be accepted.*

Still, even with this "convenant" it would take a long time to even tensions between the Orthodox and the—not.

Chapter Seven

And so, while there was the commotion of construction and hope in Rockville, 16th and Q was deteriorating.

Besides the enlarging fear of even being there at dusk, the building was still not fully air conditioned, and where it had been installed, it was faulty. The heating was antiquated and erratic. New floors were needed in the auditorium and gymnasium, as was an elevator. The meeting rooms, already renovated once, required it again. Structural changes were necessary; the building layout had to be shifted, and visitors to the art gallery had to pass through foul-smelling handball courts.

Left to Right; Hyman Berman, Charles E. Smith, Charles Jay Pilzer.
Foreground: Samuel P. Cohen

From the desk of...

CHARLES E. SMITH

(Notes for a future memoir?)

The question of the sale of the Jewish Community Center was thoroughly discussed. The need of the downtown building cannot be determined until at least one year after the opening of the new building. The Jewish Community Center as an autonomous agency will make its recommendation as to the sale to the Greater Washington Jewish Community Foundation, which will ultimately make the final decision. Inasmuch as the building will be deeded to the Foundation, the proceeds from the sale will go to the Foundation.

It was approved that we incorporate in the plans the addition of one squash court and health club facility only as an alternate bid (in the Rockville facility). The final decision, whether we actually build them, will be made by the Campaign Cabinet Committee or its successor, the Executive Board.

P.S. The health club was built towards the end of the construction period.

August 22, 1990

Dear David,

In August of Nineteen Hundred and Sixty-six I said to the Board:

> "The Health Club members have been dissatisfied with the facilities. They complain a good deal, but most do not relate to any other part of the Jewish community. Of the 254 members, only 149 contributed to UJA; only 24 of these gave pledges on the Blue Card (Fundraising)."

I told them that a question has been raised as to whether the new building will include a Health Club. Since there is so little cooperation with the rest of the Center program and no interest in supporting other programs of great worth and validity to many more individuals, the Building Committee, chaired by Abe Pollin, has decided to design a Health Club on an alternate basis. Only if the money is raised, will it be built.

My Grandson, it is a good thing we decided to go ahead with it! What use it has gotten over the years—and additions, too!

Love,
Papa Charlie

Chapter Eight

1967

The Greater Washington Jewish Community Foundation Building Committee

Mr. Robert H. Smith, Chairman

—◦◦◦—

Mr. Leonard Abel

Mr. George Hurwitz

Mr. Richard Kirstein

Mr. Ralph Ochsman

Mr. Abe Pollin

Mr. Harold Pollin

Mr. Julius Sankin

GROUND BREAKING — A DREAM BECOMES A REALITY

AND NOW WE BUILD

Dateline—The Site, Montrose Road;
Rockville, Maryland; Sunday, June 11, 1967

Left to Right: Governor Spiro T. Agnew of Maryland, Hyman Berman,
Mendel Gusinsky and daughter, Charles E. Smith, Stuart Kogod

Under a brilliant sky with bands playing and flags flying, over 1,000 people attended the Foundation's Ground Breaking Ceremony for the new Hebrew Home for the Aged, the Jewish Community Center, and the Jewish Social Service Agency.

The ceremony began at 1:00 P.M. Chairman David Lloyd Kreeger presided. The Military Color Guard from the Pentagon presented the colors and the Winston Churchill High School Band from Potomac, Maryland played the National Anthem.

This wonderful group of young musicians also entertained the audience before the ceremony. The Rabinnical Council of Greater Washington and the Washington Board of Rabbis sent representatives to officiate for the prayers of Consecration and Benediction. Rabbi Gedalia Anemer and Rabbi Merele E. Singer were chosen to represent the Washington clergy.

Charles E. Smith, Foundation President, paid tribute to the community and the spirit of dedication and foresight that had brought them to this event. A distinguished group of dignitaries extended greetings: the Honorable Walter N. Tobriner, Commissioner, Washington D.C.; the Honorable David Scull, President, Montgomery County Council; the Honorable Gilbert Gude, United States Congressman from Maryland; and the Honorable Joseph Tydings, United States Senator, and the Honorable Daniel B. Brewster, United States Senator, both from the State of Maryland.

The keynote address, which was to have been delivered by Governor Spiro T. Agnew of Maryland, was instead printed by the Foundation in "The Jewish Week." On the podium, the Governor limited his remarks to a few words, "in view of the 90 degree heat," and suggested that his audience read his seven page prepared text "in the cool of your homes."

In his speech, Gov. Agnew cited the works of Maimonides, Jewish philosopher of the 12th century: "The eighth and most meritorious step of all is to anticipate charity by preventing poverty….the very essence and the goals of the community complex that will rise on this site correspond to this thesis."

The actual ground breaking ceremony followed. Hyman Berman, President of the Hebrew Home for the Aged, was assisted by Mendel Gusinsky, oldest resident of the Home. Charles E. Smith, President of the Jewish Community Center, was assisted by Polly Garfinkle, youngest Center member. Jac J. Lehrman, President of the Jewish Social Service Agency, was assisted by Mr. & Mrs. Albert Palia, most recently naturalized Americans.

Left to Right: Vivian Rabineau, Stuart Kogod, Charles E. Smith. Groundbreaking, JCF Rockville Complex, June 1967

The Executive Directors of the agencies, Samuel Roberts (Hebrew Home), Robert Weiner (Jewish Community Center), and George Pikser (Jewish Social Service Agency) were also on the dais.

Coordinator of the entire event was Mrs. Morton Rabineau, Executive Director of the Foundation. The members of the Ground Breaking Committee were: David Lloyd Kreeger, Chairman, Stanley Rosensweig, Co-Chairman, Hyman Berman, Jac J. Lehrman, Joel Kaufmann, Mrs. Edmund Dreyfuss, Mrs. Joseph B. Gildenhorn, and Mrs. Fred Israel.

As knowledge of the campaign elevated to chatter in the community, more individuals and families started to follow its progression; naming opportunities at the Complex were successfully solicited—and in many forms: from volleyball courts to dance, ceramic and art studios; game and nursery rooms; exercise, weight lifting, first aid, mail, stage dressing, and administrative areas; lobbies, youth and cultural wings; galleries, libraries, elevators, rabbi's offices, chapels, snack bars, and a barber shop; volunteers' offices, locker rooms, an arts lounge and a cultural wing; a lake, softball fields, handball courts; medical and bookkeeping offices, a gift shop and a kitchen.

At the Jewish Social Service Agency, a plethora of persons underwrote the construction for the library, psychiatric offices, family and marriage counselor offices, family and group treatment rooms, infant nurseries, dental, podiatry, and eye, ear, nose and throat clinics, an adoption waiting room, therapy spaces, and a clients' waiting room.

The Hebrew Home was designed so that a variety of living arrangements was possible: efficiencies, one bedrooms, and doubles. On Spring Road, most of the residents had shared quarters because of little space and lack of money.

These modern nursing facilities had doctors on staff, living and dining areas, solariums, beauty shops, a snack bar, and a covered, ground-floor walkway that connected to the Jewish Community Center. Residents could buy a "Golden Age" subscription that cost $5 per year, and attend some events without charge.

The other membership levels were also conceived to be economical:

$85/Family/year.

$100/Supporting Member/year (provided funds to the JCC without actually joining).

$30/Individual for Women/year.

$40/Individual for Men/year.

$20/Youth/year.

September 1967: $6,100,000 has been raised. $400,000 left to go. It will have to come from additional solicitations from Board members.

In November, with much help from Hebrew Home President, Samuel P. Cohen, six Washington financial institutions—along with Madison National Bank—loaned the Foundation $3.5 million without any collateral—except the amount of campaign money committed to pledge cards.

Chapter Nine

The Mood of the Country

1968

Mrs. Morton Rabineau
DIRECTOR, GREATER WASHINGTON JEWISH COMMUNITY FOUNDATION

COMMITTEES

Mr. Robert H. Smith,
BUILDING

Mr. Samuel P. Cohen,
FINANCE

Mr. Norman Bernstein,
ART

Mr. Morton Funger,
FURNISHINGS & EQUIPMENT

Mr. Simon Hirshman,
LEGAL

Mr. Charles E. Smith,
AGENCY PRESIDENTS, DIRECTORS, JOINT PLANNING

Cohen and Haft;
Barbara Dorn Associates, Inc.
ARCHITECTS

Frederick Construction Company
GENERAL CONTRACTOR

Shefferman & Bigelson,
ENGINEERS

Foundation Forum Newsletter
Mrs Morton Funger
& Mrs. Joseph B. Gildenhorn
EDITORS

Mr. Ivan Chermayoff
DESIGNS FOR THE COMPLEX

Mr. Stanley Rosensweig
PLAQUES

Mr. Robert Parks
INSURANCE

Mr. Alvin Brown
ALLOCATIONS

Mr. Balfour Goldman
OFFICE SYSTEMS

Mrs. Alma Gildenhorn
DEDICATION GALA

Mr. Robert Kogod
PERSONNEL

Mrs. Barbara Landow
HISTORIAN

My grandfather believed the Jewish Community Complex should be a *tour de force,* and because of that philosophy, every single detail was pondered and planned—with precision.

He hired Ivan Chermayoff, a graphic designer from New York, to fabricate the logo, and retained the best architects: Cohen and Haft from Washington, and Barbara Dorn Associates Inc., from San Francisco. Papa Charlie inspired or mentored the most qualified community volunteers to assist him. And, with each accomplishment, the Campaign's profile rose, enthusiastically.

As "Rockville" rose to the sky, 16th and Q inched to marginalization.

The War of the Races had caused riots in Washington. Whole areas around the Center were destroyed, looted or burned, and some of its visitors were mugged.

Almost immediately the Board resolved to sell the building after the Rockville JCC opened.

But a small group called Jews for Urban Justice (JUJ) was against this strategy because of the prospective loss of a Jewish presence in Washington. They persuaded the Board to postpone the transaction, to ensure that the JCC would be placed in the custody of a purchaser more to their liking.

In September, the Center's Board transferred all of its properties — 1529 16th Street, N.W., 1518 Q, 1522 Q, and 1524
Q — to the Foundation.

A month later, the Hebrew Home and Jewish Social Service
Agency buildings on Spring Road were sold for $1,300,000
in cash. Net proceeds after expenses were $1,142,916.54.

Chapter Ten

1969

The Jewish Community Foundation
invites you to be present with
The Vice President and Mrs. Agnew
at the
Dedication Ball
In honor of the President of The Foundation
Charles E. Smith
and to salute the Jewish Community of Greater Washington
Saturday evening, the fourteenth of June
at eight o'clock
International Ballroom, The Washington Hilton

Please reply
by enclosed card

Black Tie
Reception at eight o'clock
Dinner at nine o'clock

After 44 years in the District, the Rockville Jewish Community Center was opened on May 9th. The Jewish Social Service Agency was inaugurated on May 19th and the Hebrew Home on May 20th. Each would hold a 99-year lease and a 99-year option with the Foundation, commencing on June 1, 1969; the annual rent would be: $1.

And with those rites-of-passage, the activities flowed in the three buildings; at the Center there were athletic and co-educational athletic games, cooking, sewing, wood-working, interior decorating, investments, travel, Braille, library services, pre-retirement planning, leadership development, a Center Volunteer Corps, dances, concert and theatre tickets, cultural outings, educational seminars and field trips.

Members could also participate in music, musicals, drama, and dance; weight lifting, trampoline, golf, judo, swimming, and fencing.

And, an artist-in-residence program was planned to bring eminent Jewish writers, professors, and other educators to Washington.

There were 14,000 dues-paying members from all over the

June 15, 1969, JCF Rockville Complex dedication.

area— almost immediately — with a waiting list of thousands more. Soon, the Center was attracting 50,000-60,000 visitors per month.

In preparation for a weekend of June events allotted to the Dedication, approximately 10,000 invitations were mailed; 5,000 showed for the festivities. Opera impresario, Robert Merrill performed, Supreme Court Justice Arthur Goldberg spoke, Maryland Governor Marvin Mandel welcomed the crowd, and Rabbi Joshua Haberman issued the benediction.

Left to Right: Joseph Gildenhorn, Vice-President Spiro T. Agnew, Alma Gildenhorn, Charles E. Smith, Gerald Wagner. Washington Hilton Hotel, June, 1969 Gala, Dedication of the JCF Rockville Complex.

111

Dedication Ball

SATURDAY, JUNE 14, 1969

INTERNATIONAL BALLROOM
THE WASHINGTON HILTON HOTEL

Program

Robert H. Smith, Toastmaster

WELCOME

THE INVOCATION
Rabbi A. Nathan Abramowitz

A SON'S TRIBUTE

RESPONSE
Mr. Charles E. Smith

THE INTRODUCTION
Mrs. Joseph B. Gildenhorn
Chairman of the Dedication Ball

THE ADDRESS
THE VICE PRESIDENT OF THE UNITED STATES

THE BLESSING
Rabbi Harry Kaufman

MEYER DAVIS AND HIS ORCHESTRA

DÉCOR BY THE HECHT COMPANY

My grandfather presented symbolic keys to the three agency presidents: Bernard White of the Center, George Hurwitz of the Hebrew Home, and Richard England of the Jewish Social Service Agency.

Left to Right: Bernard White, Charles E. Smith, Richard England, George Hurwitz. Symbolic Keys, Dedication of JCF Rockville Complex

The Hebrew Home and The Jewish Social Service Agency were having the same quality of success as the Center.

Later, during a few moments of quiet, Papa Charlie and Vivian Rabineau talked about what they had achieved alongside 800 volunteers.

Left to Right: Justice Arthur Goldberg, Charles E. Smith, Senator Abraham Ribicoff.
Dedication of the Hebrew Home of Greater Washington, June 1969.

"Charlie, everyone knows that without you, this could never have been achieved. You taught the community how to give. No one else could have done that with more integrity."

"Nor could I have done it without your help," Papa Charlie told her. "You did the work of four men. I really believe that G-d meant for us to fulfill this dream together."

⬥

114

Eight percent of the Jewish community had contributed to the Campaign, and retail companies from all over Washington had also aided it by contributing services at an extraordinarily high level, with sponsors such as Bristol-Myers Company, Fleischmann's Margarines, The Hecht Company, Jelleff's, Milton S. Kronheim and Company, Inc., Lorillard Corporation, Magnavox Consumer Electronics Company, Marriott Corporation, The Progress Club of Washington, Shelby Williams Industries, Inc., The Washington Coca-Cola Bottling Co., Inc., Washington Gas Light Company, Madison National Bank, The National Bank of Washington, National Savings and Trust Company, Riggs National Bank, and Suburban Trust Company of Hyattsville, MD.

Left to Right: Bernard L. White, Charles E. Smith, Maryland Governor Marvin Mandel, George Hurwitz, Richard England. Dedication of Rockville Complex, June 1969.

Other gifts came from The Association of D.C. Liquor Wholesalers, Beitzel, Capital City Liquor, Forman Brothers, Globe Distributing, International Distributing, and Washington Wholesale Liquor.

On June 15th, Dedication Day, The Jews for Urban Justice picketed in a nearby parking lot, but they had no influence then or — later — in finding a future buyer for 16th and Q.

Out of deference to the Health Club devotees, the Foundation sold the Center to the District government for $960,000 with an understanding that it was to be used as a neighborhood recreation center.

The net profit of $839,683.64 was used to help pay off a portion of the debt in Rockville.

But, according to Robert Weiner, the District reneged on its promise. 16th and Q went to Federal City College instead.

In 1985 the building was abandoned.

Dear David,

And that was it. I handed everything over to young leadership. My work was done. Although our goal had risen again—this time to $7,500,000, we were only $590,000 short. But I was confident that Vivian and all of the people who had helped us could raise the necessary money.

And we did.

For me, it was time to go back into the community to find another worthwhile project. I didn't know it would take three years.

In the meantime I kept busy, very busy.

Love,
Papa Charlie

Part Two

Back to the Community

*A good man leaves an inheritance to
his children's children.*

...an ancient proverb

The Ad Hoc Planning Committee of The Jewish Day School

Dr. Harvey Ammerman
Mr. Norman Bernstein
Mr. Herschel Blumberg
Dr. Norman Drachler
Mrs. Alma Gildenhorn
Mr. Robert P. Kogod
Mr. Julius Levine
Mr. Harry Plotkin
Mr. Morris Rodman

Ex-officio members
Dr. Leon Gerber
Mr. Bernard White
Mr. Paul Berger

Special Consultant
Rabbi Matthew Clark

In 1972, the United Jewish Appeal asked my grandfather if he had interest in helping to establish a Jewish Day School for grades K-12. At the time, a Solomon Schechter School existed, but it consisted only of seven students. The other alternative was The Hebrew Academy, which was Orthodox.

He told them he would participate on the condition that the new school welcomed all Jews: Orthodox, Conservative, Reform, unaffiliated, and non-practicing.

Papa Charlie's Jewish education had been truncated by circumstances, and then practically discontinued, until he started to think more about Judaism and Jewish survival during the years he became active in the community. By the finish of the Rockville Campaign, he was a devotee of Jewish philosophers, Jewish heroes, and classic works of non-fiction.

He became the chairman of the Jewish Day School's Facility Planning Committee. They selected a site on East Jefferson Street — across from the Jewish Community Center.

After some study, the committee estimated it would cost $2.7 million to build a school to accommodate a potential maximum of 500 students.

Papa Charlie, as was his custom, researched what he believed he could raise, by making a list of potential donors, and inking in the amounts he believed they should contribute. His determination: $2.2 million.

Papa Charlie informed my father, "I am not going to proceed with the building unless the United Jewish Appeal (UJA) contributes $500,000."

My father advised him to discuss the matter with them. Papa Charlie explained the situation to the executive director, who countered my grandfather's proposal with the question: "How are you so sure that you can raise only $2.2 million?" "I just know that is all I can raise," Papa Charlie said.

After weeks of committee ruckus, UJA finally agreed to give the $500,000, provided that my grandfather raised his share.

Papa Charlie soon reasoned that his $2.2 million alone would be worthless because it wouldn't cover the costs of

running the school, so he asked the agency for the agreement to be confirmed in writing. "Don't you take our word for it?" they asked.

"I would prefer it in writing," he said.

After the promise was made, Papa Charlie started the Day School Campaign with Vivian Rabineau. He knew it would be difficult because Washingtonians favored public over parochial schools, but he hoped that once he made an exemplary philanthropic gift—as he had during the Rockville campaign—that others would follow.

During the first campaign dinner in May of 1975, Papa Charlie expressed his views about the importance of a Jewish education. "I believe that the survival of the Jews will not depend on Orthodox, Conservative, or Reform Judaism, but on Judaism or no Judaism. A people without a tradition is a people without hope," he said, noting the huge deficit of knowledge among the general Jewish population about their history, culture, tradition, and values.

In the end, $2,190,000 was contributed. Papa Charlie returned to UJA and said the remaining $10,000 would have to come in small amounts from the community. With that, the organization gave him the $500,000, and Papa Charlie and his committee proceeded with the plans for the school. The groundbreaking occurred in March, 1976, and the building was completed in December.

January 30, 1977 was the first day of class.
The main building was named in memory of my
grandmother, Leah M. Smith, who had died in 1972.

The school started with approximately 200 students, and a standing maximum prediction of 500 pupils within five years. But by February of 1978, more space was already needed; 14,000 square feet was added to the existing 42,000 in the fall of 1979.

In October of 1980, the school's Board of Directors voted to rename The Jewish Day School of Greater Washington, The Charles E. Smith Jewish Day School of Greater Washington (CESJDS).

Dear David,

I was overwhelmed when the Board decided to name the school after me. When I first heard about it, I had tears in my eyes—and they stayed there when I had private moments with myself.

How I wished my mother and father could have been there the day of the ceremony. Not only wouldn't they have been able to imagine it, I couldn't imagine it! So many of my dreams have come true and this is because I never lacked confidence in myself. I have also had a strong belief in G-d, which has carried me through many difficult and joyous events.

I want you to always believe in yourself, my Grandson. You must have self-confidence. You should have confidence! This will enable you to make the miracles you imagine in your mind to come true.

I wish this for you more than anything.

Love,
Papa Charlie

Now, Papa Charlie desired to hone CESJDS, as it was known, into the model for Jewish education in the country by creating — for it — the most innovative, significant, and meaningful curriculum.

And so, he queried rabbis, college presidents, and experts in religion and education; none of them moved him because their thinking appeared too narrow. He decided the Jewish Theological Seminary in New York had a natural symbiosis with the Day School because it was one of the most important centers of Conservative Jewish thought in the country.

Papa Charlie contacted his friend, Gershon Cohen, Chancellor of the Seminary. Soon after, they met in Florida. Cohen told him the Seminary had never been engaged in a project such as this, but after discussing it with his faculty he said, "I want three years to work on this project with your school. The cost will be $180,000."

"You have it," Papa Charlie said. "My family foundation will supply you with a grant so that there will be no cost to the school."

And so the Seminary and CESJDS started working side-by-side in 1979 on what would become known as The Staff Development and Professional Growth Project, later renamed The Charles E. Smith Excellence Program for Day School Education.

After their visits to the school, the team formulated a route of learning that would revitalize teacher training, establish a graded course of study in Judaism, integrate different subjects, provide ritual instruction, and offer workshops to Board members and parents by Seminary professors and other scholars.

The new program was so successful that it was duplicated by the Seminary in other Jewish day schools throughout the country. And, with that breakthrough, my grandfather's third dream took formation: that the Charles E. Smith Jewish Day School breed another Maimonides.

Part Three

Shalom

⧟

God gave me the gift of life;
what I do with my life is my gift to God.

...Charles E. Smith

Charles E. Smith at his 88th birthday party,
CES Jewish Day School, 1989

Dear David,

I am overwhelmed because I will be one of the few great- grandfathers in all of Washington who can say that all of his great-grandchildren will be graduates of The Charles E. Smith Jewish Day School. This gives me the confidence to carry on, knowing that there will be Jewish continuity in the coming generations of our family.

To them I say:

Stacy, Michael, Alexandra, and Max: I love you, I love you, I love you, I love you. I want all of you to know that I will be here forever watching, observing, and guiding you, your parents, and your parents' parents.

Don't ever forget it.

Love,
Papa Charlie

Epilogue

December 1, 2008

Dear Papa Charlie,

I know you are still here; I can feel it.

And so can the community you loved. No one has forgotten you. Many people may not realize you dropped a successful career as a builder at the age of 66 to become a full-time philanthropist, but they know you dedicated your days— and sometimes nights—to helping people and organizations.

Even after your extraordinary triumphs of forming the Jewish Community Center Complex and the Day School, you never ceased to widen your humanitarian arc.

I see your name in many places, but it is the memories of you which will surely remain.

You taught—by example—the young Jewish leadership of the 1960s how to become stimulated by a cause and give to it.

That generation, in turn, rolled those lessons over to their children.

Today, Alexandra and Max's friends—though only teenagers—may not recognize your face, but they are familiar with your principles, morality, fairness, and love for all people.

You have instructed three generations within a community about tzedakah. This is amazing because when you came to Washington, there was no philanthropic profile.

I think you were sent by G-d to achieve this miracle.

Love,
David

Appendix I

Recently, THE CHARLES E. SMITH JEWISH DAY SCHOOL was rated by *The Jerusalem Post* to be one of the top five Jewish schools in the world.

It is now comprised of two campuses:

> • *The Lower School,* grades K-6; 750 students; 1901 East Jefferson Street, Rockville, MD; a third wing was built in September, 2000; a fourth addition was constructed in September, 2001.

> • *The Upper School,* grades 7-12; 700 students; 11710 Hunters Lane, Rockville, MD; opened in September, 1999.

50-125 CESJDS students go to the Jewish Community Center each afternoon to either participate in activities, study, go to the teen lounge, or relax.

Meanwhile, THE DISTRICT OF COLUMBIA JEWISH COMMUNITY CENTER returned to Washington despite only scattered support from the community, and the United Jewish Appeal. My grandfather held enthusiasm for a new District of Columbia JCC, but not at 16th and Q—at first.

1985: *Jewish Community Center re-incorporates at 2027 Massachusetts Avenue, N.W. in two offices with a budget of $500,000, and a membership of 330.*

1986: *The DC Jewish Community re-opens at 2028 P Street, N.W.*

1988: *The Center relocates to 1836 Jefferson Place, NW.*

1990: *The original building at 16th and Q, now abandoned, is re-purchased from the City at a cost of $2.3 million.*

1997: *16th and Q is re-inaugurated and re-opened. The cost of renovation is $17 million. The operating budget is $3.3 million.*

2008: *Operating budget is $7.3 million; 1,800 members.*

THE JEWISH SOCIAL SERVICE AGENCY, previously at 1131 Spring Road, N.W., Washington, D.C., and incorporated on May 1, 1933, moved to its 18,160 square foot Montrose Road location on May 19, 1969. An extension edifice of 30,000 square feet was inaugurated in 2008.

THE ORIGINAL HEBREW HOME was on 1125 Spring Road, N.W., in Washington DC, from 1910-1969. It had its last structural addition in 1953 at a cost of $27,000, which increased the number of beds from 35 to 165. The 1969 Montrose Road building had 250 units; today: 556.

Since then, there have been additions to the Hebrew Health Care System:

1978: Revitz House opened.

1981: Smith-Kogod Residence constructed.

1984: Research Institute on Aging established.

1989: Ring House built.

1991: Hirsh Health Center finished.

2002: Smith-Kogod Residence renovated; re-dedicated in 2003.

2005: Landow House completed.

2006: The services of the senior homes are united under the "Charles E. Smith Life Communities" to honor the generosity and memory of my grandfather.

2008: The Homes care for more than 1,000 patients a day.

Appendix II

The Life of Charles E. Smith

1901:   *Born Lipnick, Russia.*

1911:   *Left Russia for the United States; settled in Brooklyn, NY.*

1923:   *Left accountancy position with Federation of Jewish Charities; starts his building career.*

1923-29: *Cycle One of business success.*

1927:   *Marries Leah Goldstein.*

1928:   *Robert H. Smith is born.*

1929:   *Loses money in Depression.*

1930:   *Works various jobs to support family.*

1934:   *Arlene Ruth Smith is born.*

1942:   *Moves to Washington, D.C. to resume building career; first project in Washington fails.*

1943:   *Employed as construction superintendent for the Waverly Taylor Company.*

1946:   *Forms Charles E. Smith Companies; builds apartments and office buildings in Washington, D.C., Maryland, and Virginia.*

1967:   *Retires from The Charles E. Smith Companies; becomes its Chairman of the Board and a full-time philanthropist.*

1972:   *Leah Smith dies.*

1975:   *Marries Micki Uretz.*

1995:   *Dies in Palm Beach, Florida.*

The Community Activities
of Charles E. Smith

- *Honorary President, United Jewish Appeal of Greater Washington.*

- *Member, Board of Trustees, George Washington University.*

- *Member, Board of Governors, Hebrew University.*

- *Board Member, Jewish Theological Seminary of America.*

- *Board Member, Washington D.C. Board of Trade.*

- *Past President, District of Columbia Jewish Community Center.*

- *Past President, Hebrew Home of Greater Washington.*

- *Past Vice President, United Jewish Appeal.*

- *Past Vice Chairman, United Givers Fund.*

- *Past Chairman, Construction Division of United Givers Fund Board and Health and Welfare Committee.*

- *Council Benefactor and Namesake, Charles E. Smith Jewish Day School.*

- *Chairman, Council of Advisors, Charles E. Smith Jewish Day School.*

Awards Received

1963:   *Ottenstein Award.*

1966:   *Honoree, Jewish National Fund.*

1966:   *Honoree, Jewish Theological Seminary of America.*

1967:   *Recipient, Jewish Community Center's Ourisman Award.*

1968:   *Recipient, Prime Minister's Medal.*

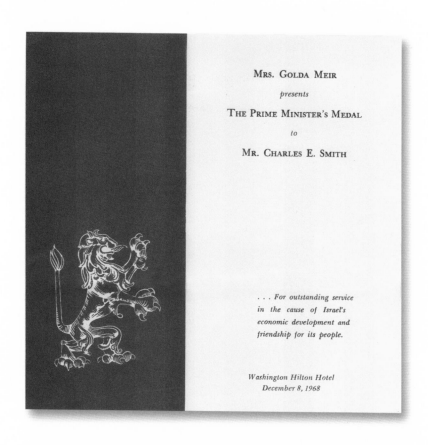

MRS. GOLDA MEIR

presents

THE PRIME MINISTER'S MEDAL

to

MR. CHARLES E. SMITH

*. . . For outstanding service
in the cause of Israel's
economic development and
friendship for its people.*

*Washington Hilton Hotel
December 8, 1968*

1971:   *Honorary Fellow, Hebrew University.*

1971:   *Recipient, B'nai B'rith Humanitarian Award.*

1972:   *Recipient, Jewish Theological Seminary's Louis Marshall Award.*

1973:   *Recipient, Hebrew University's Magnes Medal.*

1975:   *Honorary Doctor of Philosophy, Hebrew University.*

1979:   *Honorary Fellow, Jewish Theological Seminary of America.*

1979:   *Honorary Doctor of Public Service, George Washington University.*

1980:   *National Brotherhood Citation from The National Conference of Christians and Jews.*

1982:   *Doctor of Humane Letters Honoris Causa, Jewish Theological Seminary of America.*

1988:   *Honoree, Washington Business Hall of Fame.*

Bibliography

Interviews

By Adam Cohen and David Bruce Smith

Thursday, January 24, 2008:
Morton and Norma Lee Funger
Eddie Kaplan
Arna Meyer Mickelson

Monday, January 28, 2008:
Jack Cohen
Sheldon Cohen
Jill Moskowitz
Robert Weiner

Tuesday, January 29, 2008:
Richard England
Arlene Kogod
Geraldine Nussbaum

Wednesday, January 30, 2008:
Joseph and Alma Gildenhorn
David Osnos
Clarice Smith
Robert H. Smith

Books

Smith, Charles E., Smith, David Bruce, and Muller, Peter, *Building My Life; Privately Printed: 1985.*

Smith, David Bruce, Conversations with Papa Charlie: A Memory of Charles E. Smith, *Capital Books: Sterling, VA, 2000.*

Archives of Charles E. Smith, Volumes 1-5; 1957-1983.

Papers

Benor, Roberta, *"The Jewish Community Center of Greater Washington, 1958-1983: Twenty-Five Years of Service,"* 1983.

Mihm, Stephen A., *"Maintaining a Jewish Presence in the Nation's Capital: The Debate Over the Location and Function of the District Jewish Community Center,"* July 19, 1993.

Weiner, Robert H., *"The Jewish Community Center of Greater Washington, 1958-1983—Years of Change,"* 1983.

Mrs. Joseph B. Gildenhorn, Mrs. Morton Funger, Editors; *"The Foundation Forum,"* September-October, 1967.

Board Meeting Minutes of The Jewish Community Center, 1964-1968.

Footnotes

[1] *Most of the quoted statistics come from papers written by Stephen A. Mihm, Roberta Benor, and Robert H. Weiner. See bibliography for additional details.*

[2] *Stephen A. Mihm, "Maintaining a Jewish Presence in the Nation's Capital: The Debate Over the Location and Function of the District Jewish Community Center," July 19, 1993, p. 7.*

[3] *Mihm, p. 9.*

[4] *Robert H. Weiner,* "The Jewish Community Center of Greater Washington, 1958-1983—Years of Change"; *1983, p. 6.*

[5] *Mihm, p. 14.*

[6] *Roberta Benor, "The Jewish Community Center of Greater Washington, 1958-1983: Twenty-Five Years of Service"; 1983, p. 5.*

[7] *Weiner, p. 9.*

[8] *Benor, pp. 5-6.*

Benor, Roberta, *"The Jewish Community Center of Greater Washington, 1958-1983: Twenty-Five Years of Service"; 1983.*

Mihm, Stephen A., *"Maintaining a Jewish Presence in the Nation's Capital: The Debate Over the Location and Function of the District Jewish Community Center"; July 19, 1993.*

Weiner, Robert H., *"The Jewish Community Center of Greater Washington, 1958-1983—Years of Change"; 1983.*